# Regaining Focus
# During a Global
# Pandemic

## FANTASIA ROBERTS

Written by Author,

and manuscript completed © 2020.

Front cover photo was purchased and licensed on Fiverr by Rebeca-Ira P.

Scriptures from the Holy Bible.

Webster Dictionary online was used.

Contributors to writing:

Devin Gay

Tonya Bostick

Joy Bookhart

DeDe Harris

# DEDICATION

This book is dedicated to everyone who feels like giving up. To the one who feels like they're alone and that nothing in life is turning out the way it should. To anyone who's ready to throw in the towel. I implore you to read this book and to know that you are not alone. Whatever it is that you're going through, whatever obstacle you're faced with, whatever the situation may look like GOD is turning it around for your good. Don't give up and don't look back, just keep moving forward. You don't have to face this journey alone! You will be ok! God is turning it around for your good! You're not what people call you! You are a child of the KING. I want you to remember that you have the Power to take your life back. You have the Power to get everything under control, again. What you can't do, is fix it ALONE. Give it to GOD and let it GO!

# TABLE OF CONTENTS

Dedication

Acknowledgments

# ACKNOWLEDGMENTS

All thanks and praise belong to God. For He is the head of my life and this book would not have been possible without Him. I thank Him for the gift of writing and being able to share with the world just how great He is. I would like to thank my children; Tamara, Nevaeh(deceased), Katelynn, Morgan, Wilton Jr, and William Malachi. You all inspire me to be great. You keep me focused and sane when I feel like the whole world is crumbling at my feet.

I'm thankful for the journey of heartache, pain, child loss, and failure. In ways these things shaped me into the woman I'm becoming. Last but certainly not least I would like to thank Tonya Bostic, Dede Harris, Devin Gay, and Joy Bookhart. You all provided me with insight and different perspectives on the word Prayer. For that, I'm grateful. You were patient with me even if at times I seemed a bit demanding. You guys ROCK!

# Chapter 1
# The Process

The year had just started, and as always my new year's resolution was the same as every year before. Don't be in the same place this year as you were last year. For me, that meant mentally, physically, spiritually, and emotionally. However, this year (2020) would prove to be different. As we all know this year we were faced with a world pandemic and everything around us would begin to change.

How could I find myself? How could I take control back over my life? How could I move forward, when everything around me was falling apart? For me, and my family I needed to find ways to remain calm and try to hold on to the little sanity that I had left. Not just for me, but also for the little people looking up to me.

Though the process had already proved to be hard enough, I had to dig deep. I had to face everything that held me back or caused me to be stagnant. This would mean confronting my past as well as my present. So, let's begin. Over these past few years I've lost some really important people in my life.

-August of 2009 I loss my daughter Nevaeh

-May of 2016 I loss my biological father

-January of 2017 I loss my maternal grandmother

-July of 2017 I loss my father in-law

-May of 2018 I loss my uncle Mack, who reared me as his own

During these untimely events each person took a piece of me. With each piece that was taken, I became lost, confused, bitter, and miserable. Let's call it how it is, I was becoming someone I no longer recognized when I looked in the mirror. Who was this woman? Where had Fantasia gone? The loss of these people did something to my mental state. I didn't realize that emotionally I was still dealing with hurt from my childhood.

That physically I looked for a man that would validate who I was. That spiritually, I yearned for a closer relationship with God. However, I was afraid of what other people may think. That mentally, I wasn't altogether! I was still angry with God for taking my daughter away. I had to face all these things on top of a failed marriage. Before 2020 I didn't have to, because I had so much going on in life that I had other things to focus on. I had an outlet, I could shift my mind to something else and not deal with the current. But now, I have time to think, reflect, and get myself together. This year would be the process in which I healed. During a pandemic at that! Regardless of how hectic, painful, and disturbing as this year would prove to be. I needed to go through THE **PROCESS**! This year I would implement **P.R.A.Y.E.R.** because nothing else was working. I needed to go back to my roots.

**P**- process/pray

**R**- release/repent

**A**- acceptance

**Y**- yearn

**E**- evolve

**R**- repeat

Webster gives the definition of **process** as: "a natural phenomenon marked by gradual changes that lead toward a particular result."

However, biblically **<u>my process</u>** would follow some of the same steps just in a different manner.

1) I would have to go through the same stages as the "OLIVE" in order for my anointing to present itself and for me to flow. Not just in the natural realm but the spiritual realm as well. I needed to be shaken, beat, and pressed. Not physically, but I needed to be prepared for my destiny. My mindset would need to change, I would need to reconstruct how I approached situations, and take a look at my atmosphere.

Though the beginning of this process would seem more difficult than the end, I needed to start somewhere. I felt that praying would be a good start. However, I needed to remember how to pray! What would I say to God? How could I come before God and say I was ready to change, again? He had heard this from me before. The process is what I needed to tackle, head on.

I had a way of going to God when I felt it was beneficial to me. Then when I did something I was ashamed of, instead of praying, I hid. I was like Adam and Eve when they ate the forbidden fruit. Instead of going to God and acknowledging

my faults and wrong doings, I tried to hide. Who else has hidden from God in shame? Did you stop praying because you felt He wouldn't listen? Did you continuously do the thing you told God you wouldn't do anymore? How do you deal with guilt? What process did you take to change? What process would you like to start to change?

Not for me, or anyone else but YOU! For me, to begin the process, I would start on my knees in **P.R.A.Y.E.R.** Praying does something for me spiritually. Crying out to God for forgiveness and help; does something for me mentally and emotionally. It releases something in my spirit and also in the atmosphere. It's like me coming to God about everything that's bothering me. Telling Him about all my problems, worries, and concerns. Instead of trying to do it alone!

## Chapter 2
## Releasing Myself and Repent

The next step of my **_process_** would be to **RELEASE**! **Release** some things and people whom I've allowed to have authority over my life. Sometimes, we give people power without knowing that we're giving them power. We allow what others think of us to dictate how we move. Letting go can be hard, however, sometimes it's NECESSARY. The very thing that we hold on to could be what God is waiting for us to **RELEASE**.

Webster gives the definition of **release** as: "to set free from restraint, confinement, or servitude".

Whew! That alone can be hard to do. We become so accustomed to patterns that we can easily lose ourselves. We can be in bondage and not even know it. Once something has control over your life to you it may seem like the "NORM." What's been holding you HOSTAGE, who's been holding you HOSTAGE? Have you not become tired yet?

Are you comfortable? Is this what you want for your life? I hope not! I'm tired of being boxed in, I'm tired of feeling like I owe everyone something, I'm tired of giving more time and effort to people than I give to God and myself. I'm ready for a **RELEASE**! I'm ready to LET GO! I don't want to stay confined to the thought process of someone else. 2020 would be the year I release and renew all things in my life. Though we're coming to the end of the year it's not too late to start. Starting now is better to not start at all. What are you **RELEASING** yourself from in 2020?

During the **RELEASE** process I would need to come to the realization of what's really important and what's not. Who needs to stay and who do I need to let go of? This for me was extremely hard. It caused me to re-evaluate friendships and even my marriage. As much as we hate to admit it, some people are only meant for seasonal purposes. Just like seasons change, so do we. We outgrow people and certain environments. We have to **release** ourselves from certain patterns that could possibly be hindering us from reaching our full potential. **Releasing** or letting go is hard, I used to do everything possible to see or create a different perspective of situations I had faced. My marriage failed, I was ashamed. I wanted to stay, I wanted to make it work, I needed our children to see that mommy and daddy were ok. I wanted the two parent household for my children because it's something I didn't have. But, should I stay just for that reason? Should I stay so that the kids could be tucked in bed by both parents at night?

Should I stay because I felt like if I left it would be too heartbreaking for the kids? Or, should I **RELEASE** myself from it? Not because I got tired of my marriage, but because we outgrew each other. We were on two different wavelengths! Just like when you're at the beach and you see a surfer trying to catch that next big wave, if you're not an expert in surfing sometimes you get caught in the wave.

I wasn't an expert in my marriage, and you don't have to be. But, I got caught in the thought pattern that if my marriage didn't work God wouldn't forgive me. However, I no longer wanted to move in a circular motion and continuously repeat the same cycle. The wave moves the particles of water in a circular motion, and the current moves the water in a direction. I was headed in a different direction, we both were. And, that was okay! I just needed to find the courage to **RELEASE** myself from what I thought my life should look like; and allow God to have complete control and guide me into who I was destined to be. Again, **RELEASE** is hard, but it's NECESSARY!

Now, I know it's hard sometimes to take advice from others, I used to be the same way. But, when life has knocked you down and you still muster up the strength and courage to push forward it says a lot. Oftentimes, we don't talk with others, such as friends, family, or our significant other when we're battling with things. That's because we don't want to impose our misery or problems upon others. However, sometimes it's okay not to be the strong one all the time.

It's fine if you need an outlet to just express and be free. Free from judgment, fear, and feeling less than. Once I got to the point where I was comfortable with who I was becoming, my process didn't seem difficult at all. However, once I release myself from people, places, and things I need to go back before God and repent. Webster gives the definition of repent: "to feel or express sincere regret or remorse about one's wrongdoing or sin".

I needed to go back to God, I needed to make Him the head of my life again. I needed Him to know that I was sorry. I was sorry for doubting who He was. I was sorry for doubting what He was capable of. I was sorry for putting people and things before Him. I was sorry for cursing Him. I was sorry for straying away. I was sorry for neglecting my calling and who He had destined me to be. Biblically, repent is "a call to persons to make a radical turn from one way of life to another".

What dead weight would I be letting go of? What ways would I need to change? Living in the natural realm while trying to keep one foot in the spiritual world was becoming clearer to me. Like the old folks say "I was trying to straddle the fence". My aunt Gwen and uncle Mack used to always have these conversations with me.

Truth be told, at 33 years old my aunt still does. She always says "Tasia you can't keep living two lifestyles" and she was right. Even though I don't want to admit it to her. It takes a lot out of me to admit when I'm at fault. I'm learning, that's part of my process. Nonetheless, I was releasing and repenting!

## Chapter 3

## Accepting My Faults

The next step of my process would be **<u>ACCEPTANCE</u>**. I stepped on my own toes when I got to this step. This is the part of the **process** that I had to really reflect on. Why is that, you may ask? **Acceptance** would mean that I had to take accountability for my part and not just pass the blame onto others.

Webster defines **Acceptance** as: the act of accepting something or someone-the act of being accepted (APPROVAL).

This word can go different ways in the process! I can't count the many times I've accepted something that I shouldn't have. When you find who you really are, tolerating anything from anyone is no longer acceptable to you. You've managed to find YOU and you're learning to love the person you've become. With loving the person you've become you no longer look for approval from your peers.

Biblically speaking **_ACCEPTANCE_** is:"embracing the reality of a situation based on one's trust in God's perfect will and control. So, for me that would mean no matter how tough things became I would **accept** the hand I'm dealt and trust that God is in control. That no matter what situation I was faced with NOTHING was too hard for God. That I could **accept** my failed marriage, that I could **accept** the loss of my daughter, that I could **accept** losing people whom I love, that I could **accept** anything and continue to push forward.

Please understand that even though we **accept** some changes and events that take place in our life doesn't mean we're okay. It simply means that we've **accepted** the fact that things happen, whether good or bad, but we trust God. How many times have we questioned God about something that's happened in our life? I know I have countless times.

Is it ok, no? Does God understand, yes? Why? Because we're human, and it's an instinct to point a finger when something bad happens; or doesn't go the way we want it to. I've **accepted** the fact that I'm not perfect and I make mistakes. I've also **accepted** the fact that I can't do this alone. I need God in my life, I need Him head of my life, I need to take a backseat and let God drive. Why? Every time I've taken the wheel away from Him my roadmap in life has become blurry. I get confused about which direction to go. I make wrong decisions and when I go back and try to cover it with a bandaid, I just make a bigger mess out of the situation.

This year though, in this season, God I give you COMPLETE CONTROL, I can't fight these battles alone. _**Acceptance**_ can also be hard, but it's Necessary. What are you **accepting** today? What are you giving God control over? It's hard to say you've **accepted** something and still complain. Why complain if you've given it to God, fully?

There's no need to, He has our back when we don't have our own. This process started off hard but the more I seek change, and become a better version of myself, the easier it gets. When you shift your way of thinking change comes about.

# Chapter 4

## My Desire to be close to God

**_YEARN_** would be the next step of my process. Because I desired a closer relationship with God. I wanted Him more than I think I ever wanted Him. I longed for Him, I cried out to Him. I knew that during this process; I had tried to handle everything thrown my way, like a Champ. I tried my way all along. I had been doing it wrong though, I had been trying to navigate this life of mine, on my Own.

Not looking to the one who created me in His image. I was creating a bigger mess than what was needed. It wasn't until I got to my lowest point that my thoughts began to change. Isn't it funny? We can cry out to God and pray when we need Him. What happens during the times that we're showered with His blessings? Do we just need to forget about Him? Do we praise Him, or ourselves? Truth be told, if it wasn't for God on our side where would we be?

Webster defines the word yearn as: to long persistently, wistfully, or sadly.

This can be translated in different ways in the natural realm. When those close to me began to pass away; I longed to hear their voice, see them smile, wrap my arms around them, and express what they mean to me. Eventually, I began to come to terms with their passing, but I still long for them. I wish I had more time with them. Biblically speaking the word yearn is: to stretch out to reach after.

I had come to that point. I had navigated in all the wrong directions until I navigated myself to the truth. I needed God and the more I reflected on my life the more my hunger grew. I was in search of ways to be fed the Word of God. I picked up my Bible and began to read it more often. Then, I found myself reading it everyday. I began to call upon others who were grounded in the word. Those who Faith had been shaken, those that would guide me properly, those who saw my desire and wanted me to grow more spiritually.

## *Yearn has 4 occurrences in the Bible*:

*2 Corinthians 9:14* "while they themselves also, with supplication on your behalf, yearn for you by reason of the exceeding grace of God in you."

*Philippians 1:8* "For God is my witness how I yearn over all of you with tender Christian affection."

*Genesis 43:30* "Joseph hurried, for his heart yearned over his brother; and he sought a place to weep. He entered into his room, and wept there."

*Deuteronomy 28:32* "Your sons and your daughters shall be given to another people; and your eyes shall look, and fail with longing for them all the day: and there shall be nothing in the power of your hand."

While each scripture gives different perspectives of yearn, whether it be that of the natural or spiritual they counteract each other. Sadly enough I had given my all, at least that's what I thought. My battles were becoming more than I could bear. I needed help! So, in this step of my process I began to let go of my desire for what man could give me and focus on what I had in Jesus Christ. Who I was becoming in Him was more important than who I was in the past. I was learning what the true desire of my heart was. That was to have a closer relationship with God and not let anything or anyone intervene.

The flesh is hard to deal with when you have so many temptations and obstacles set before. However, everything that the enemy meant for my bad God was turning it around for my good. I could've been pulled out this rut a long time ago, but I had a way of blocking my own blessings. My yearn had become stronger this year and I was ready to move forward.

# Chapter 5

## Evolving and transforming

The next step of my process would be to **Evolve**. I had implemented the *process*, I *released* things that had been holding me back, I *accepted* me for who I was, and the fact that I couldn't face this journey alone, I had begun to *yearn* for a deeper and closer relationship with Christ, and I was finally beginning to *evolve* into the woman God destined me to be. However, when I started to evolve I needed to change my thought process.

I had to learn my worth and who I was in God. *Genesis 1:27* states that "So God created mankind in His own image, in the image of God he created them; male and female he created them." So, why do we settle for less? Why do we allow others to dictate who we are and what we can do? *Jeremiah 29:11* states: "For I know the thoughts that I think toward you, saith the LORD, thoughts of peace and not of evil, to give you an unexpected end." While I began to evolve and my thought process changed I was finally beginning to walk into my destiny. Things that I allowed to hinder me no longer kept me in bondage.

Webster defines evolve as: "to produce by natural evolutionary processes."

So, in the natural realm, I was changing my thought process, my environment, and how I handled situations. I was determined to become a better version of myself daily. Why daily? Because I knew that I wasn't going to get it right every day. I knew that some days were going to be better than others.

However, I had little people looking up to me and counting on me. My biggest fans called me "MOMMY" and I couldn't let them down. Biblically speaking the word evolve means: renew and transform. **Romans 12:2** says: " Be not fashioned according to this world; but be ye transformed by the renewing of your mind. That ye may prove what is the good and acceptable and perfect will of God."

During this process a transformation had to take place. I didn't have to become someone I wasn't, I didn't have to try and fit in, I didn't have to walk in a path of what others thought of me, I didn't have to talk like someone else, I didn't have to dress like someone else. All I had to do was simply be me.

In my first book Chapter 33: Piece by Peace I wrote a poem entitled: *Imperfections*, and in that poem I talk about feeling like I wasn't good enough, trying to fit into society, hiding my flaws, and at the end I gain confidence in who I am as a person.

## IMPERFECTIONS

How can you just stand there and pretend like you don't see it?

Come closer, do you see it now?

All those imperfections

You know you'll never be good enough

And there I was face to face

Examining her from head to toe

Basking in the simplicity that I could never be her

She was amazing

Head held high

If I didn't know any better, I would say she had her face in the clouds

She had confidence for miles

Miles that only she could travel because there was no way I could fill her shoes

Here I was plain Jane

Just an ordinary girl

Trying to find my place in society

Using make-up to hide my blemishes

So, I could make up for those imperfections

Applying my massacre

so, the mask that I wore day to day

wasn't so easily portrayed

That's why my favorite brand was Maybelline

Because maybe I can find a glimpse of me in her

In doing so maybe I would discover my self-worth

Because I'm not her

and society has placed so many standards on who I should be

when all I should have to be is me

No, I'm not perfect

If you can't love me for me then leave me be

I'll never be who you would like me to be

That woman I examined

Face to face

Was it a replica of me?

I was fixated on who society wanted me to be

My two-way mirror shattered

Honestly, I don't want to stay stuck in this pattern

Head held high

Confidence obtained

My imperfections no longer am I ashamed

I'm just an ordinary girl

With extraordinary capabilities

Learning to bask in the simplicity of being me…

Evolving, transformation, growth, or whatever term you would like to use when becoming a better version of yourself; is much like the butterfly. The butterfly has 4 life stages that take place:

1) the egg is laid

2) the larva (caterpillar) hatches from the egg

3) the pupa (chrysalis) is the developing stage of the butterfly, where the wings begin to form underneath the skin. This is the stage in which the butterfly hides itself before merging into this beautiful creature.

4) the butterfly emerges.

How long are you going to hide yourself? When will you emerge? God did not create us to hide in the image of someone else. He didn't create us to be followers! He created us in His image! We all have a calling, we have a purpose, we can change, we can make a difference. It's never too late to grow or evolve into the person you're meant to be.

When 2020 began, I had no clue what the year would hold for me and my family. I didn't know if I was going to remain stagnant or break the cycle. I had no clue that we would be faced with a global pandemic. However, I made the decision to change. No one forced me into change, and I can't force you to change. What I will tell you though is that we weren't created to struggle, we weren't created to live in the shadows of someone else.

For most of us, the change has begun; and if you're like me, you're scared. You don't know if you can do it alone, you may lose some friends, people may talk about you. So what! Let them talk! If you lose friends let them GO! I challenge everyone who reads this book to let go of what's been hindering you from prospering and reaching your full potential. If it's not helping you to progress and move forward, let it GO! I'm ready to see some BUTTERFLIES!

## Chapter 6

## Repeat, Replay

We've come to the end of our process, what a journey. But, you made it. Look at where you were in the beginning and look at you now. The glow up looks good on you. I know this wasn't easy, it was hard for me to. I didn't think I was capable, but I was determined to change. I was determined to get my life back on track. I needed a fresh start. There is no turning back now.

Will all days be good days? Maybe not, but you have control over how your day begins and how it ends. If the first thing you do when you wake up is say "today is not going to be a good day" then 9 times out of 10 it won't be. Instead, pray when you wake up. Create the day you would like to have. Change your thought process. When you think positive thoughts, negativity really has no room to enter. If it tries, just say "Not Today Satan". My challenge to you is to try and implement the steps I took to regain my focus during this difficult time. Life gets busy, and whether it be work, school, children, friends, or family it seems like it's not enough hours in the day. During the most hectic of days, that's when you need to find time to breathe. Even though we all try to wear capes, we can't be superheroes all the time. However, there is a God that sits high and looks low, who's our Superhero today, tomorrow, and forever more.

Prayer really does change things. If you have to repeat and replay the steps everyday until it's a part of your thought process do so. Make it a lifestyle! I didn't want this process to just be what **P.R.A.Y.E.R** meant to me because I value the opinions of others. So, I asked a few co-workers. I gave them each a letter from the word **P.R.A.Y.E.R** and here is what they had to say.

**Devin-** Prayer is our first line of communication with God. It means full vulnerability whether right or wrong.

Devin is absolutely correct, the communication we have with God is like no other. When we can't go to friends or family about our problems or situations that we face we can always go to God.

**Tonya-** "Becoming a better version of yourself in the image of God. To stop searching for love, friendship, family acceptance, and putting myself last. Molding myself by listening to the Word and living it as well. Letting my purpose that God has already bestowed in me manifest. God speaks to me with whispers of all the things I could be working on, yet I'm in my own way."

*Psalms 119:4* "Thou hast commanded us to keep thy precepts diligently."

*Psalm 119:5* "O that my ways were directed to keep thy statutes".

*Psalm 119:6* "Then shall I not be ashamed, when I have respect unto all thy commandments."

*Psalm 119:7* "I will praise thee with uprightness of heart, when I shall have learned thy righteous judgements."

**Moral:** "I can not and will not have what's for me unless I believe myself as God believes in me."

Tonya is striving to be better today than she was yesterday. It's amazing how our circumstances and environment can change when we read the Word of God.

*John 14:6* says: "I am the way and the truth and the life. No one comes to the Father except through me."

How awesome is it to be able to go before God? When life is going good or when it's not so good. We can go to God and give thanks and to ask for guidance. Everybody has a different story, but the God we serve covers us all.

**Joy-** "Acceptance is an understanding that you have not just with yourself, but with God. It's something that comes from within. It's a part of healing! A lot of it has to do with Faith as well. If your Faith is strong then you will be more accepting of things that may be harder to accept (like, things you can't see or feel). Once you accept God into your life you accept all the blessings and Faith that comes from Him."

Wow, we all know that accepting things we don't like is hard. But think about it! God still accepts us when we're wrong. He still loves us in spite of our flaws. He still offers us forgiveness when we do wrong. Joy mentioned Faith a few times. In **Hebrews 11:1** it says: "Now Faith is the substance of things hoped for, the evidence of things not seen."

Are we able to accept the things we can't see? Are we able to push forward when we feel like giving up? Yes, WE CAN! We're able to accept and move forward because our Father in heaven sits high and looks low. He's promised to never leave nor forsake us.

**DeDe**- Release for DeDe was to "let go and let God have His way. Regardless of everything going on, continue asking for God's will to be done".

That's powerful! Sometimes we get so accustomed to people, things, and places that we overlook or don't realize when it's time to move on. We like to call it our "Comfort Zone"! But, when are we going to step outside that zone? What will it take to say you've had enough? Sometimes,

God removes us from familiarity to unfamiliar. In doing so, he gets us out of the relaxed stage.

The stage where we think we know everything. He makes us uncomfortable. We need to be uncomfortable at times. It's during those times that our belief began to align with our Faith. We know who God is, we know what he's capable of. However, there are times where God needs to show you that "it was Him". Not man, not woman, not family, or friend. That situation seemed too hard to face? Don't worry God is in control. Didn't know how your bills were going to get paid? Don't worry, God made a way.

Prayer and Faith is key. When I started to write this book I already knew I wanted insight from these individuals. Why? These four inspire me and they don't realize that they're inspiring me. We all vary in age and while our end result is ultimately the same. Our outlook is a bit different!

This is just a way of showing you that no matter how old you are, how many times you've failed, how many times you didn't give something your all. It's never too late for change. Repeat and replay and make today a better day. You got this! We got this! You're not alone! Remember that the battle is not yours to fight, it's the Lord's. In whatever you do please remember to implement:

Process/pray

Release/repent

Acceptance

Yearn

Evolve

Repeat and replay


Again, I look forward to seeing BUTTERFLIES emerge! Even in the midst of a global pandemic. Regain focus and take your life back.

"For I know the thoughts that I think toward you, saith the LORD, thoughts of peace, and not of evil, to give you an unexpected end."
*Jeremiah 29:11*

## CONTRIBUTING WRITERS

### Devin (NOT PICTURED)

### Tonya

### Joy

### DeDe

"For I know the thoughts that I think toward you, saith the LORD, thoughts of peace, and not of evil, to give you an unexpected end."
*Jeremiah 29:11*

## ABOUT THE AUTHOR

Fantasia is a mother of five: Tamara(13), Katelynn(10), Morgan(9), Wilton Jr(6), and William Malachi(2). She loves her children, and is willing to sacrifice anything that she can, to ensure they have a quality life! She decided this year to complete her writing projects. Her first book, *Piece by Peace*, will give you insight to just some of her struggles.

However, in spite of her struggles, she's chosen to regain her focus in life; even during this pandemic. She's an unselfish person, and upon completing this project, she wanted to get some insight from her coworkers. Fantasia has turned to God in prayer, studying her Bible and encouraging others along the way.

Though you'll read of the various obstacles she's had to face, you'll also read of her journey back to peace. The process that she had to implement while going back to her roots. Prayer has always been an evitable part of her life. For some time she strayed away from God, her belief, and the morals and values that

"For I know the thoughts that I think toward you, saith the LORD, thoughts of peace, and not of evil, to give you an unexpected end."
*Jeremiah 29:11*

had been instilled in her. This journey takes her back to cope and accept her past. However, it gives her the strength she'll need to endure the present and her future. What the devil meant for bad in her life when she decided to dedicate herself and family back to God, it's all been turning around for her good. In the words of one of her favorite singers: Fantasia was *"**gracefully broken.**"*

She may have been bent, but she didn't break; because her trust has and always will be in the Lord!

Made in the USA
Columbia, SC
22 November 2022

71600376R00024